Paris, Tightwad, and Peculiar

T0170841

Project Sponsors

Missouri Humanities Council and the National
  Endowment for the Humanities
Missouri State Library
Western Historical Manuscript Collection,
  University of Missouri–Columbia

Project Directors

Susanna Alexander
Rebecca B. Schroeder

Consultants

Virginia Lee Fisher
Donald M. Lance
Adolf E. Schroeder
Arvarh E. Strickland

Special Thanks

Patti Dudenhoeffer
Dealia Lipscomb
Howard Marshall
Adult Learning Center, Columbia
Daniel Boone Regional Library, Columbia
Missouri Folklore Society
SERVE, Callaway County
State Historical Society of Missouri, Columbia

Missouri Heritage Readers

General Editor,
REBECCA B. SCHROEDER

Each Missouri Heritage Reader explores a particular aspect of the state's rich cultural heritage. Focusing on people, places, historical events, and the details of daily life, these books illustrate the ways in which people from all parts of the world contributed to the development of the state and the region. The books incorporate documentary and oral history, folklore, and informal literature in a way that makes these resources accessible to all Missourians.

Intended primarily for adult new readers, these books will also be invaluable to readers of all ages interested in the cultural and social history of Missouri.

Books in the Series

Paris, Tightwad, and Peculiar

MISSOURI PLACE NAMES

Margot Ford McMillen

UNIVERSITY OF MISSOURI PRESS
Columbia and London

Library of Congress Cataloging-in-Publication Data

McMillen, Margot Ford.
    Paris, Tightwad, and Peculiar : Missouri place names / Margot
Ford McMillen.
        p. cm. — (Missouri heritage readers)
    Includes bibliographical references (p.) and index.
    ISBN 0-8262-0972-6
    1. Names, Geographical—Missouri—Juvenile literature.
2. Missouri—History, Local—Juvenile literature. I. Title. II. Series.
F464.M36 1994   94-25468
977.8—dc20   CIP
                                                              AC

∞™ This paper meets the requirements of the
American National Standard for Permanence of Paper
for Printed Library Materials, Z39.48, 1984.

Designer: Kristie Lee
Typesetter: Connell-Zeko Type & Graphics
Printer and binder: Thomson-Shore, Inc.
Typefaces: Palatino and Birch

The publication of this book has been supported by a grant from

MISSOURI
HUMANITIES
COUNCIL

To Howard, Holly, Heather, Sandy, and John

Contents

Acknowledgments

———————⇒✥⇐———————

Writing this book has been great fun, mostly because it's given me the chance to work with and talk to many fine people. Some of my debts have accumulated over a long time. Don Lance has been clarifying and correcting my understanding of language for years. With this manuscript, he was particularly helpful and read it several times as I revised. Other acquaintances were brief, like those with my fellow sandbaggers at Rocheport one dawn during the flood of 1993. As the sun came up, we entertained each other by telling how our hometowns got their names and watched as the Missouri River crept to its crest. This reminded me how important place names are and how much our everyday history means to us.

So thank you, Don Lance, and thank you, sandbaggers. Now I'll try to list the rest. I owe a huge debt to Dolf Schroeder for photos from his "Missouri Origins" collection, his considerate suggestions, coffee, and cookies.

I also want to thank my good friend, Tina Hubbs, who has read copy, made indexes, numbered pictures, and generally kept me on track with this and other projects over the last years. Dennis Murphy, our favorite illustrator, has made maps and drawings for Missouri Interpretive Materials for years. Some of his work appears in this book. And my husband, Howard Marshall, is always my first reader and commentator.

Many other people have read this manuscript in its various stages: students and tutors from the Adult Learning Center in Columbia and from SERVE in Callaway County, consultants, and other participants in the project. Archivists from the State Archives, the State Historical Society of Missouri, and many collections across the state have helped me find photos and drawings to illustrate the ideas.

Most of all, of course, I want to thank the collectors and writers who have thought about place names over the years. Robert Ramsay, Charles van Ravenswaay, Gerald Cohen, and others—I know you only through your writings, but I feel we have met. Thank you.

Paris, Tightwad, and Peculiar

Present-day Missouri counties.

1

The Name Game

These towns have Peculiar Enough names.

—Headline, *Columbia Missourian*, March 17, 1981

Before there were counties or towns, roads or railroads, or even a state of Missouri, there was a land with hills, streams, and rivers. In the forests, giant pine, oak, and hickory trees were home to deer, turkey, and songbirds. The tall prairie grasses provided shelter and food for buffalo, rabbits, and elk.

Today, the land has been packaged for human convenience into counties, cities, and towns; there are hundreds of divisions. All of them have names. All of the rivers, streams, lakes, hills, roads, and highways have names, too. Each of these names has a history.

Some of the place names are odd. "Tightwad" is the name of a town in Henry County. A tightwad is a miser, a person who rolls his paper money in a tight wad so that he can put it in his fist and hold onto it. According to the legend, the name comes from the first store owner in the area, back when the town was called Edgewood.

They say that the store owner sold a beautiful sixty-pound watermelon to a mailman for $1.50. This was back when mailmen still took the mail around in buggies or horse-drawn wagons. The store owner was happy with the price and agreed to keep the melon until the mailman passed by again on his way home.

Pretty soon, however, a city fellow in a car came by. He offered the storekeeper $2.00 for the melon. The storekeeper had no trouble making up his mind. He sold the melon and got another one from his garden for the mailman.

When the mailman came back and saw the new melon, he knew it was not the one he had paid for. He was angry. He took the smaller melon, but as he drove away he shouted as loudly as he could, "Tightwad! Tightwad!" People say this is how the town got its name.

A place name has important meaning. When you hear

(Dennis Murphy drawing for Missouri Interpretive Materials)

the name, you see the place in your mind. For places that you don't know, a name may remind you of stories about it. So, if you want people to think you are careful with your money, you may want to open an account at the Tightwad Bank. Many people have done that, just to have the name "Tightwad" printed on their checks.

A place name is like a little record of history. Over the years, a name may remain even after the place changes. The wolves have disappeared from Wolf Island in Mississippi County, and the elk have left Elkland in Webster County, but the names remain.

Early explorers needed place names to tell each other where there were good campgrounds or hunting spots. One hunter could have said to another, "I saw a buffalo on the path that leads to the river." If more buffalo were seen there, the spot could become well known. One hunter could say "Buffalo Place" or "Buffalo Path," and the others would understand. If someone built a store nearby and a town grew up, the town could be called Buffalo.

There are twenty-five places in Missouri named for the buffalo, including Buffalo Creek and the French "Boeuf Creek," both in Franklin County. However, there are many ways a place can get its name. The town of Buffalo in Dallas County may have been named by settlers from Buffalo, New York.

Some place names came from people who were having fun with words. Sharp, in Ozark County, was named for a trader who was sharp enough to get the better of another. Shake Rag in Warren County was named to make fun of the ragged clothes of the early settlers. A school in Franklin County was called Reed's Defeat for a man named Reed, who was the school's first teacher. He had so much trouble with the older boys that he lost his job.

The Accident School was established in 1894 about ten miles
southeast of Cassville. The last log school in Barry County,
it was open until 1915. School board records show that the
name was chosen when the school first opened, but the board
didn't record the story behind the interesting name. (State
Historical Society of Missouri)

Many small towns were named by people who wanted
to bring a post office to the community. If they wanted
mail delivery, they had to think of a town name. In 1886,
the Post Office Department in Washington, D.C., asked
that new town names be short—just three letters. Missouri
towns named "Map," "Nip," and "Not" were all approved
that year.

In Shannon County, one little town was having no luck
in finding a name. The neighbors met to discuss the problem. They found a spelling book with three-letter words in
it and began to read. Bat? Cat? The meeting dragged on

until somebody spilled a bottle of ink on the table. The problem was solved. "Why not call the town 'Ink'?" The name was not in use any other place in Missouri, so the new post office was in business.

Now, this is a good time to mention something about place-name stories. Not everyone agrees on all the details of each one. In fact, people around Ink have several explanations for the name. One person said that the postmaster named the town just after receiving a shipment of goods that had been spoiled by a broken bottle of ink. Another said that the postmaster wrote down all the three-letter words he could think of and sent the list to Washington, D.C. The Post Office Department chose the name from his list. Which story is right? You can take your pick.

Another Shannon County town was named by a frustrated postmaster who first suggested the names of his daughters. He tried to name his post office after Edith, the eldest. The post office department wrote that there was already an Edith in the state. Next he tried Ethel; that name was already in use. He tried Alice, but there was already an Alice, Missouri. Finally, he did what many of us want to do when we're dealing with the government. He wrote "Rats!" on the application form and sent it in. This name was approved, but the post office shortened it to three letters: Rat, Missouri.

The Post Office Department has been blamed for many odd names. Another postmaster, in Iron County, sent in 200 names for approval before finally calling his town "Enough."

Some odd place names came about by mistake. The people of Plad in Dallas County wanted their town to be named "Glad," but the post office printed the name wrong, and it was too much trouble to get the mistake corrected. People decided to go ahead and call the town "Plad."

In place-name stories, time sometimes rewrites history. There are two stories about the name of one of our most peculiar town names—Peculiar, in Cass County. The earlier story, recorded in 1929, says that some settlers were looking for a farm. Coming over a hill, their leader exclaimed, "That's peculiar! It is the very place I saw in a vision in Connecticut." They bought the farm and built a town, naming it, of course, "Peculiar."

Another story says that the town was named by a tired postmaster who sent many applications to Washington. One by one, the names were rejected. Finally, he asked the Post Office Department for help and was told to try something new or "peculiar." No matter which story you believe, you can pass through Peculiar, Missouri, when you travel in the western part of the state.

Some people think that the Maries River was named after two girls named Mary or Marie. This is not true. Early maps show the Maries River marked "marais," which means "marsh" or "swamp" in French. Maries County was named for the river.

Some people have said that the Ozarks was the place where Noah's Ark landed after the flood. However, the name comes from the early French explorers. They wrote "aux arcs" ("at the Arcs") on their maps to indicate where the Arcansa people ("arcs" for short) lived or hunted. When the French said "aux arcs," it sounded like "Ozark" to English speakers. Many places in Missouri now have the word *Ozark* or *Ozarks* in their names, including a county, a town, and the hills themselves.

In Missouri, it was common for a name to be used by one group, then changed in some way by others. Sometimes, as in "marais" and "aux arcs," spelling and pronunciation changed when the new group started using the name. Sometimes only the pronunciation changed. Even our state name is pronounced in different ways: Is it Missour-uh or Missour-ee? According to Don Lance, a professor of English at the University of Missouri–Columbia, "Missour-uh" was once the most common pronunciation, but now "Missour-ee" is the most common in all areas of the state except the northwestern part. Both are correct, but—sad to say—young Missourians are abandoning the older pronunciation.

Missouri places have been named by all kinds of people— Native Americans, French explorers and settlers, German immigrants, pioneers from the British Isles, and freed African American slaves. Each place name tells us something about the people who settled there. Settlers bring their own ideas to a place, and they name their towns to remind themselves of the homes they left behind or to show their hopes for the new land.

2

---·>●<·---

Native American Place Names

If all other textbooks were lost entirely, we could recover most . . . recorded history by studying our place names—and also a good deal of . . . history that has never been recorded.

—Robert L. Ramsay, *Our Storehouse of Missouri Place Names*

The first people to see the land we call Missouri were descendants of people who came from Asia to North America a long time ago.

Some scholars think the first crossing from Asia might have been 50,000 years ago. Others say it was 30,000 or 20,000 years. Probably, the first Americans walked across ice or a land bridge from Siberia to the area that is now Alaska. The place where they crossed is now called the Bering Strait, and today it is full of ocean water.

We know very little about the early explorers. They shared the land with mastodons and giant sloths, but what kind of language did they speak? How did they live? What were the paths they took as they settled throughout North and South America? We don't know because so many years

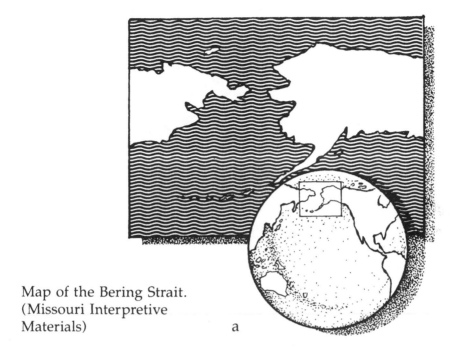

Map of the Bering Strait.
(Missouri Interpretive
Materials)   a

have passed. Most likely, these first human explorers had
names for the landmarks—rivers, hills, caves, and lakes—
but we don't know the names they used. There was no
writing to save the names for the future.

We do know that they were good survivors. They fished
and hunted by hand and with spears. They knew how to
treat animal skins to make shoes and clothing. They found
new plants and animals to eat and new materials to build
with. They learned to use natural plants and animal parts
as medicines. They passed knowledge from elders to children by showing and telling. Stories and songs were handed
down from the old to the young. Skills such as hunting,
cooking, making pottery, and building fires were taught by
demonstration.

Over the years, the native population grew in number.

By the time Europeans came to North and South America, the Native Americans lived in all parts of the western hemisphere. Some lived in groups of families, and some of these groups formed nations extending over large areas. The European explorers called the people they found here "Indians" because they believed the land was part of Asia.

About 12,000 years ago, people began wandering in and out of the area we now know as Missouri. If food was scarce in one place, the people would travel by boat or on foot to another. Each group probably named landmarks in its own language. Native Americans often gave places two names. One was sacred and not shared with outsiders. The other described the place for everyday conversation.

The first Missourians used stone tools. Over the years, many groups of people lived in the region. New groups came with new skills as the old groups disappeared. (diorama at Mastodon State Park, photograph Missouri Interpretive Materials)

Finally, some tribes settled and made their homes in the area. Each group brought new skills—pottery making, weaving, food preservation, and farming. They traded with other tribes and brought new things into the villages. By the time European explorers came, the Osage in our area were growing corn, potatoes, squash, pumpkins, and beans.

Groups of Osage said their names in different ways, and the names were hard for white men to say and write. Explorers Lewis and Clark called the Osage "Wasbasha." Other explorers spelled the name "huzzah" and "hoozaw." So we have Huzzah Creek in Crawford County and Hoozaw River and Whosau Trace in Warren and Saint Charles counties. The French called the tribe "Osage" and gave the name "Osage" to the river where they lived. Today, several places in Missouri have the word *Osage* in their names, including a county and a town by the river.

Most of the words used by the Native Americans are lost. Only a few words have been saved, written on the early maps and in journals by European explorers. These words, which usually described places, have become place names in our language. Two of these are "Neosho" and "Niska."

Neosho is a river and town in Newton County. The word *neosho* described a river. It means "clear springs" or "main river." The Niska is also a river. Its name means "white river."

Another name from the Native Americans is "Nodaway." The original meaning is unclear. The word *nodaway* might mean "quiet water" or "water crossed without a canoe" or "snakes, enemies." Whatever its meaning, the name "Nodaway" has been given to a river, a county, and townships in five counties. People like to use a lovely word like *nodaway*, even if they don't know what it means. A nineteenth-century poet wrote about the many Native American names of rivers and streams in the United States:

. . . mid the forests where they roamed
There rings no hunters' shout;
But their name is on your waters;
You may not wash it out.

—Lydia Huntley Sigourney
(1791–1865), "Indian Names"

There are other names that probably came from native words, but their meanings have been lost. *Pemiscot*, for example, might mean "liquid mud," or "runs next to." Either description fits the muddy swamp next to the Mississippi River in southeastern Missouri's Pemiscot County.

The Osage name for God remains as a place name long after the Osage are gone. It comes to us as "Wakenda" or "Wyaconda," names of places in Carroll and Scotland counties.

The Sauk, the Fox, and other tribes from Illinois left their names on many Missouri places. Kahoka in Clark County was a campground for one branch of the Algonquins, who came across the Mississippi River in the late 1700s. A word sounding like "monito" was the Algonquin word for "spirit." Spelled the French way, Moniteau, it became the name of a mid-Missouri county and river. From the Sauk Indians we have the name of the highest peak in Missouri, Taum Sauk. The meaning of *taum* is a mystery. It may be a version of *tongo,* the Sauk word for "big."

Some place names use words that were borrowed from Native Americans in New England and traveled to other parts of the country as pioneers moved west. How do we explain names like "Moccasin Hollow" and "Moccasin Springs"? In New England the word *moccasin* was borrowed into English to refer to a kind of shoe. The word was also used for an American snake with stripes that look like the seams on moccasins. When the first white settlers came to Missouri, they used *moccasin* in names for places where they saw that kind of snake or for places where they thought nothing but moccasins could live. So "Moccasin Hollow" in New Madrid County and "Moccasin Springs" in Cape Girardeau County are names that follow the naming traditions of white settlers rather than Native Americans.

3

———⟫●⟪———

The French Explorers

The joy that we felt at being chosen for this voyage made us feel brave, and the work of paddling from morning to night felt good to us.

—Father Jacques Marquette

The word *history* refers to stories of events, usually written down, and *pre* means "before." So we call the time before books and writing "prehistory." In America, prehistoric times ended when the first European men visited and wrote about the land and people. European maps and journals give us the earliest place names we know.

The journal of Father Jacques Marquette, a French priest, is one of the first written records about the Mississippi River. With a French explorer and trapper named Louis Jolliet and five Native American guides, Marquette came down the Mississippi from the north in 1673. He wanted to teach Christian ways to the native tribes. His government also wanted him to look for gold and other valuable resources.

Marquette and Jolliet planned for their trip a long time. They had lived with native tribes for two years. The Native

14

Americans knew this region because they had hunted and fished up and down the rivers and streams.

Marquette had learned seven native languages. There were no maps of the river, so he made his own for the trip. "We got all the information we could from the Indians who had travelled in that region," he wrote, "and we even traced out from their reports a map of that new country; on it we wrote the names of the rivers, and the names of the peoples and of the places we were to pass."

Marquette and Jolliet began their journey on May 17, 1673. The explorers traveled in birch-bark canoes made by their guides. Travel was dangerous any time of the year, but they hoped that if they left in the spring they could return before winter.

When Marquette returned home, he wrote a journal of his trip. He described the places along the river, trying to remember and copy the words used by his Native American guides. The guides called the river they explored "Mississippi." That means "big river." When they met another large river coming from the west, the guides called it "Pekitanoui." "Pekitanoui is a river of great size," Marquette wrote, "coming from the northwest, from a great distance. It empties into the Mississippi." Later French travelers gave Pekitanoui its present name—the Missouri River. The word *pekitanoui*, which means "muddy river," has disappeared, but the river is still sometimes called by its nickname, "Big Muddy."

Missouri is a French version of a Native American phrase. It's the name the Illinois Indians used for the people who lived and hunted west of the Mississippi River and north of the Missouri River. It means "big canoe people." Other tribes were amazed by the Missouri tribe's large canoes, which were dug out from giant cottonwood trees. To those

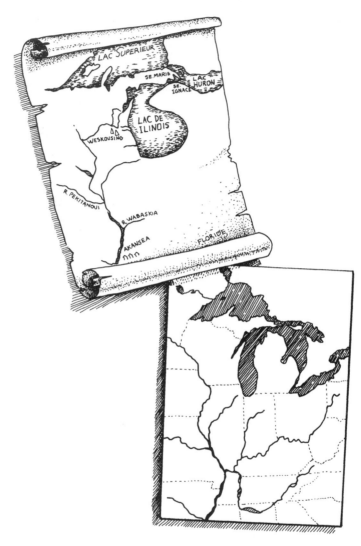

Map drawn by Father Jacques Marquette and modern map
of the same area. Marquette made his map from the descrip-
tions of his guides and from his own observations, trying to
record the names used by his Native American guides as they
described the waterways to him. Today's mapmakers use
photographs from airplanes and satellites to show the exact
locations of lakes, rivers, and land formations. (Missouri
Interpretive Materials)

using light, birch-bark canoes, the heavy dugouts looked huge.

Marquette saw few people on his journey. The Native Americans may have been hiding from the strange white men and their guides. But there was another reason that Marquette saw few people: even as early as 1673, the Native Americans in the region were disappearing. In some places, large villages stood empty. The people may have died from diseases or may have been killed in battles with other tribes. Some migrated to other areas for reasons that we may never know.

Many explorers followed Marquette and Jolliet and reported that the land had beautiful forests and prairies, plenty of game to hunt, good waterways, and rich lead mines.

Early French explorers named the rivers and creeks they found, so knowing the meanings of a few French words helps us understand these names. The Current River in southeast Missouri, for example, is probably named for the French word *courant*, which means "swift-running water." *Platte*, the name of a river in northwest Missouri, means "shallow." *Saline* in central Missouri means "salty."

The word *femme* means "woman," so the creek "Femme Osage" must have been named for an Osage woman or princess. *Loutre* is the French word for "otter." Loose Creek was called "L'ours Creek" by the French, "the bear creek." The Americans called it "Loose Creek" because they didn't know French, and the name "loose" seemed to fit a creek that sometimes flooded the countryside.

The Gasconade River, first named "Blue River," was hard to navigate. To travel 150 miles, a boatman had to wind through 500 miles of sharp turns and rapid waters. It was, in the words of Dru L. Pippin, a blustering and

This photograph of the Mississippi River was taken at Trail of Tears State Park. The park was named for a trail used by Native American tribes when the U.S. government moved them from their native lands in the East to reservations in the West. They suffered many hardships on the journey. (Missouri Division of Tourism photo)

boastful river. "That's me," it seemed to say, "the Gasconade, a true-blue, one-hundred-percent Missourian!" The Ozarks' Blue River was renamed "Gasconade" for the rich region of Gascony, France, where people were known for bragging and teasing their neighbors.

4

The First French Towns

In the name of the most high mighty Louis the
Great . . . I . . . do now take, in the name of his
Majesty . . . possession of this country of Louisiana.

—Robert Cavelier, sieur de La Salle

In 1682, a French explorer named Robert Cavelier, sieur
de La Salle led fifty-two other explorers, hunters, and guides
down the Mississippi River from Illinois to the Gulf of
Mexico. La Salle claimed all the land west of the Mississippi for King Louis XIV of France and named it "Louisiana" for the King. La Salle dreamed that there would soon
be French villages on both sides of the Mississippi River.

The first settlement in Upper Louisiana grew around the
lead mines in present-day Ste. Genevieve and Washington
counties. As early as 1720, about 200 workers, including
many black slaves, began to work the mines. The mining
companies shipped the lead down the Mississippi River to
New Orleans.

The lead-mining area is still called Missouri's mineral region. Most mineral-region towns were once mining towns.
The town called Mine La Motte in Madison County is a

reminder of the early mines. It was founded by Antoine de la Mothe Cadillac, governor of Louisiana, and named for him in 1714. La Mothe's last name, Cadillac, is well known today. Exploring Michigan in 1701, he founded Detroit. His name was given to another settlement (Cadillac, Michigan) and much later was used by General Motors for its elegant and expensive car.

In 1724, a French explorer, who had been named commandant of the Missouris by his government, built a fort on the Missouri River in today's Carroll County. Etienne Veniard de Bourgmont had visited the area earlier and was welcomed by the Missouri tribe. Soon many Native Americans moved from their camps to be near the fort. There, they found traders and soldiers to protect them from their enemies. The fort, the first in Upper Louisiana, was used for only six years. It soon disappeared, but the place name "Fort Orleans" is still on the official Missouri map, showing where a marker of the site has been placed.

Many Native Americans and French became friends. In 1725, Bourgmont took a group of Native American chiefs to France to meet the king. The Native Americans showed the king and his court how to shoot bows and arrows. They danced and sang. A Missouri chief's daughter was baptized in Paris and married a French soldier.

The people of France and the Native Americans must have thought each other strange. One Native American said later that the French women with their perfumes smelled "like alligators." The French thought of the Native Americans as wild men, or "noble savages." Neither group understood the other.

When the French settled west of the Mississippi, they named their villages in traditional French ways. Some were named after Catholic saints. Missouri's first permanent

Three Osage. By the time this drawing was made in Paris
in 1827, the Osage were giving up buffalo robes and jewelry
made of bone and feathers. They preferred European-style
woven wool blankets and metal jewelry. (photo from a tinted
lithograph in the State Historical Society Art Collection)

settlement was Ste. Genevieve. The first homes in the settlement might have been built as early as 1735. Why was "Ste. Genevieve" chosen as a name? We are not certain, but we know that it is the name of a Catholic saint who started life as a shepherd girl in the fifth century. Sainte Genevieve is the patron, or special, saint of Paris, France.

Perhaps the settlers arrived at their new home on January 3, the day chosen by Catholics to honor Sainte Genevieve. Or the name may honor an early woman settler named Genevieve. The French often named places for a person's patron saint rather than with the person's own name. Or maybe the settlers wanted to honor the city of Paris.

The town's first homes were washed away by the Mississippi River in 1785, the year of a great flood, so Ste. Genevieve was moved to a different location. Still, some of the oldest houses in Missouri are in Ste. Genevieve. The way the French built log cabins was with logs placed like posts in the ground rather than laid one on top of another to make walls. During the flood of 1993, the Mississippi threatened Ste. Genevieve again. Volunteers had to build levees with sandbags to protect the historic houses.

Ste. Genevieve also had a French nickname, "Misère." It means "misery." This nickname tells us something about life in early times. The settlers lived in small cabins with little protection from the weather. In winter, the only heat came from a fireplace. They had to make, find, or grow everything they needed. To visit other places, the settlers walked or traveled by canoe or horse.

The first Missouri road was built between Mine La Motte and Ste. Genevieve. It was called Three Notch Road. At first, the road was simply a path through the woods. To

This addition to a log cabin in Washington County shows the French method of log construction: the posts are placed upright in the earth or on a foundation. (photograph by A. E. Schroeder)

follow it, a traveler would look for trees with three cuts, or notches, on the trunk. These marked the road and gave it its name.

St. Louis, founded in 1764, was another early French settlement. It was named for the patron saint of King Louis XV. Three years after builders began St. Louis, another town was started. Carondelet was named for a governor of Louisiana. The nicknames for these towns were "Short of Bread" for St. Louis and "Empty Pocket" for Carondelet. These nicknames tell the true story: the early settlers had a hard life.

5

Towns for the Fur Trade

About the year 1719 these Indians began regular trade with the Euro-Americans. As the Indians turned more and more to the business of preparing skins for sale to these traders they gave up most of their old arts and adopted European-type weapons, tools and clothing.

—Duane G. Meyer, *The Heritage of Missouri*

Even though life for early settlers was hard, Europeans and Americans kept moving west. They came because there was a chance for a new start in the territory and a chance to get rich.

One way to make money was to trade with the Native Americans, who were good hunters and trappers. The skins of bear, deer, buffalo, and mink were sent to cities, where they were used to make expensive clothing. Beaver fur was made into hats, which were popular with Americans and were even sent to Europe.

Euro-American traders knew they could make the best deals with tribes living where white men had not gone before. They would travel the rivers and streams looking

24

for faraway Native American villages. There, they would trade European tools, guns, liquor, and beads for fur. When a trader had all he could carry, he would load his canoe and take his furs to town to sell them. Ste. Genevieve and St. Louis, both river towns, had markets for traders.

European traders brought many useful things to the Native Americans. Iron shovels soon replaced tools made of stone or bone. Wool blankets replaced buffalo robes. Hunting rifles replaced bows and arrows. And the Native Americans traded for jewelry, especially the shiny glass beads from Italy.

But some European inventions seemed useless to the Indians. When they first got brass cooking pots, they used the metal to make jewelry. They were satisfied with their handmade clay pots for cooking and storing food.

In this engraving, a Native American studies the factory-made goods offered in trade for animal skins. (State Historical Society of Missouri)

A trader named Girardeau or Girardat camped often at a rock called Cape Rock, south of St. Louis. Even though this spot was known by other traders as early as 1760, there were no houses built there until thirty years later. When settlers came to live near the camp, they named their new town "Cape Girardeau." (State Historical Society of Missouri)

In 1762, during the French and Indian War, Louis XV ceded the Louisiana Territory to his cousin Charles III of Spain. The Spanish thought the land might have valuable treasures. Many years earlier, the Spanish had settled in parts of South America, Mexico, and the American West.

Very few Spaniards actually lived in this area, and few Spanish names dating from their rule (1763–1800) remain. In 1767, a Spanish fort named for their prince was built on the banks of the Missouri River near the Mississippi. Fort

As the trade centers grew, flatboats replaced dugout canoes. A flatboat was a large raft with low sides. Sometimes it had a shelter where the boatmen could sleep. Each flatboat could carry a lot of heavy goods—mostly furs and lead—from Missouri to the East or to the South. When the boat finished its trip, the owner took it apart and sold the lumber. The crew then had to walk back to Missouri to start another trip. One of the nineteenth century's best-known artists, George Caleb Bingham, is known for river scenes like this one, *The Jolly Flatboatmen*. Bingham lived in Missouri most of his life. (State Historical Society of Missouri)

Don Carlos told the world that the Spanish were now in command of the river. The site was hard to defend, and the Spanish left the fort after only a few years. In 1769, a town was built near Fort Don Carlos on a site well known to travelers, who called it "Les Petites Côtes," or, in English, "The

Little Hills." The town was named "San Carlos" to honor the Spanish. Renamed "St. Charles," English for San Carlos, it was the first capital when Missouri became a state.

"New Madrid" was named by Colonel George Morgan, a native of New Jersey, who planned the town in 1789. Morgan wanted to establish a settlement west of the Mississippi River in Spanish territory, and he found a beautiful site in a peaceful bend in the Mississippi below the mouth of the Ohio River. It was located near a place French traders called "L'Anse a la Graisse," or "Greasy Bend." Historian William Foley explained that "Greasy Bend" got its name because "Indians often boiled down buffalo or bear grease there."

Morgan wanted to give his town a name that would please the Spanish, so he settled on "New Madrid" to honor the beautiful Spanish capital. A French mapmaker who visited the town in the 1790s renamed it "La Nouvelle Madrid," but as American settlers moved west of the Mississippi it became New Madrid again.

By 1789, enough towns had been built next to the river that there was need for a road. Using an old Native American trail, the Europeans built a road from St. Louis to New Madrid. To the traders, the road was a signal that they were taking over the land as well as the water. They gave it a grand name—"El Camino Real" in Spanish, or "royal road." The French called it "Rue Royale," but it was the Americans' name for it that we know today—"Kingshighway." Parts of the road are still in use, following U.S. Route 61 along the Mississippi River.

6

Trails and New Settlements

Every person, both French and Americans, seemed
to express great pleasure at our return. . . . They informed us that we were supposed to have been lost
long since.

—William Clark, 1806 journal entry

In 1800, the Spanish traded the Louisiana Territory back
to France. Three years later, President Thomas Jefferson
bought the territory for the United States. Jefferson was
excited about his purchase, and he asked the soldier Meriwether Lewis to explore the new land and report on his
discoveries. Lewis chose William Clark to join him.

Lewis, Clark, and a crew of explorers, including a black
slave named York, left St. Charles in 1804. They followed
the Missouri River, crossed the Rocky Mountains, traveled
down the Columbia River, and even saw the Pacific Ocean.
The safe return of the explorers made people feel that settlers could go farther west.

In their journals, Lewis and Clark described the places
and people they saw. They described the Osage people as
strong and peaceful, "the largest and best-formed Indians."

This tribe had "made advance in agriculture." They lived by hunting in spring and fall and growing food during the summer.

In their journals, Lewis and Clark told the legend of the origin of the Osage nation:

> The founder of the nation was a snail, passing a quiet life along the banks of the Osage, till a high flood swept him down to the Missouri and left him on the shore. The heat of the sun at length ripened him into a man. . . .
>
> The Great Spirit appeared, and, giving him a bow and arrow, showed him how to kill and cook a deer, and cover himself with the skin.

When the explorers' journals were published, people read about the gentle Native Americans and the rich land west

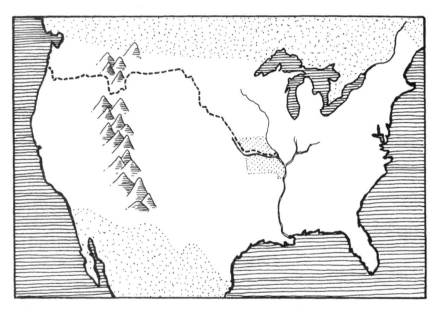

Map of Lewis and Clark's journey. (Missouri Interpretive Materials)

of the Mississippi River. The United States government offered free land to settlers, and the rush to the West began.

Families imagined that life on the frontier would be easy. With neighbors helping, they could build a log cabin in a day and a small barn just as quickly. With luck, good workers had a crop to sell in a few months.

Life was not easy for many. Epidemics of diseases like cholera, smallpox, and measles killed entire families. Bad weather wiped out crops and killed livestock. But the chance to own land continued to pull people west.

With more people in the region, river towns grew. Store-keepers opened businesses. Wagon builders, shoemakers, millers, and horse breeders came to Missouri.

St. Louis was in the right place at the right time and became a major trade center. Flatboats on the Mississippi carried lead and furs to market. From the south, traders brought cotton, sugar, and slaves. From the eastern factories came iron tools, clothing, pots, and dishes. Some of these goods were made at American factories; others came from Europe.

New resources were discovered. In 1806, Daniel Boone's sons went into business producing salt from a salty spring called a "lick," where animals gathered to lick the salt deposits that were left by water from the spring. The spring became known as Boone's Lick, and the trail was called the Boonslick Trail. Today, we still hear about the Boonslick region, which includes the towns of Boonville and Boonesboro. Part of the Boonslick Trail is still with us, running along Interstate 70 between St. Charles County and Boonville.

Settlers came to the new territory to sell resources, go into business, or farm. They hoped for opportunities for themselves and for their children. To make the settlers feel safe, the government built several forts on the rivers.

This iron kettle dates from the Boonslick salt operation developed by Daniel Boone's sons. At the operation's top capacity, the Boones shipped 100 bushels of salt per week from the spring. (State Historical Society of Missouri)

One Missouri fort was named for a woman, Hannah Cole. It was called Fort Hannah or Fort Cole. In 1807, the Cole family was traveling to Boone's Lick from Kentucky. They were attacked by members of the Sauk tribe, who stole their horses and killed Hannah's husband. She went on with her nine children and one cow and finally arrived near present-day Boonville. She built her cabin and planted corn, but for the first year the family diet was mostly wild game, acorns, and slippery elm bark. They made their clothing from animal skins.

More families came to the settlement, but the Native

Lewis and Clark had noted a good site for a fort in present-day Jackson County. In 1808, Fort Clark was built there. The name was changed to Fort Osage in 1811 because the Osage Indians had moved close to it for protection by the U.S. military. Commanded by George Sibley from 1818 to 1826, the fort's name was changed to "Fort Sibley." This fort lasted longer than any other in Missouri. A town called Sibley was later built near the location. Other forts built around this time were named for their commanders: Fort Clemson, in present-day Warren County; Fort Howard, on the Cuivre River; Fort Mason, south of present-day Hannibal. It is surprising that none of the fort names became town names, but the forts didn't last more than a few years. (Missouri Valley Special Collections, Kansas City Public Library, Kansas City, Missouri)

For a while, the graceful keelboat was queen of the river.
Up to seventy feet long, she could sail if the wind was right.
(State Historical Society of Missouri)

Americans kept attacking the settlers. The War of 1812 was raging in the East, and the American government could not send soldiers to protect the settlers in the West. Many tribes saw the War of 1812 as a chance to stop the growth of the United States toward the west.

Finally, in 1814, the settlers in Hannah Cole's neighborhood built a strong fence of logs like those used in forts. The fence, or stockade, had openings so the settlers could shoot at their attackers. They built Fort Hannah in only a week, but it was strong enough to keep them safe.

The fort was still used after peace came. It served as a community center, courthouse, voting place, schoolhouse, church, post office, and hospital.

In the years after the Lewis and Clark report, Missouri

grew rapidly. Early towns like St. Louis and Cape Girardeau became small cities.

Keelboats became common on the river. Keelboats had a round or V-shaped bottom and were more expensive to buy than flatboats, which usually lasted only one trip and then were taken apart and sold as lumber. The keelboat could carry more men and cargo and make more than one trip. The coming of the keelboat seemed to say, "Civilization is coming to the wild frontier."

7

——————⟫●⟪——————

The Earthquake and New Towns

On Monday morning last, about a quarter past two,
Saint Louis and the surrounding country was visited
by one of the most violent shocks of earthquake that
has ever been recorded since the discovery of our
country.

—*Louisiana Gazette*

In the first five years after the return of Lewis and Clark,
a number of homes were built along the Mississippi and
Missouri rivers. Then, on December 15, 1811, something
happened to change the pattern of settlement. A writer for
the *Louisiana Gazette* in St. Louis preserved the story. He
said he was awakened by the noise of shaking windows,
doors, and furniture, with a distant rumbling noise, like "a
number of carriages passing over the pavement."

The strongest part of the earthquake was near New Madrid, a village of about 800 by that time. After the first
earthquake, there were 27 more shocks before daylight.
Towns were flooded and riverboats were swamped. The
quakes went on for over a year. Not many people were
killed, but many lost their homes.

Afraid of more earthquakes, many New Madrid people

asked the United States Congress to trade their homes for new land. Because of the War of 1812, the government was slow to act. Finally, certificates were granted. Each certificate was good for 640 acres. Some people took advantage of the situation and made fake certificates. Trading in New Madrid certificates brought more people to the territory.

Many people traded New Madrid certificates for land north and west of the earthquake area. Most traded them for good farmland in central Missouri, but developers claimed some of the certificates. The early downtown area of Hannibal was claimed by developers who owned New Madrid certificates. They then divided it for sale.

The names for Hannibal and nearby Palmyra come from Roman history. Hannibal was a North African general who fought in a Roman war on Carthage, a city in North Africa. Palmyra was an oasis in the Syrian desert.

Who gave these names to Missouri places? Latin and Roman history were important subjects in early American schools. Some people think that the first surveyors in the area named the creeks for places and people they had studied. The towns later took their names from the creeks.

Another old town in the area, Port Scipio, was named for a rival of General Hannibal. Port Scipio and Hannibal were once about the same size. In ancient history, Scipio finally defeated Hannibal in Africa, but in Missouri, Hannibal took over Scipio. The Port Scipio Boat Club is all that remains of the old town.

There is another interesting story about the name "Hannibal." In his book *White Town Drowsing* Ron Powers says that Hannibal was named by York, the slave who traveled with Lewis and Clark. According to this legend, York called himself Hannibal after the African general. The legend says that York was left as a guard when the explorers left

Sketch of a flatboat moored near a house on the bank of the
Mississippi River near St. Louis on April 8, 1826, copied by
Charles Peterson from the original drawing by Charles A. Le-
Sueur in the Museum of Natural History, LeHavre, France.
(State Historical Society of Missouri)

the boats to look around. The explorers never got lost because they could hear York shouting, "This is Hannibal.
This is Hannibal."

This tale can't possibly be true. First of all, there is no
mention in Lewis and Clark's detailed journals of another
name for York; second, the famous Lewis and Clark journey took place on the Missouri River, while the city of
Hannibal is on the Mississippi.

No matter how it was named, Hannibal became an important shipping town, serving traders in canoes, on flatboats, and in keelboats. All these crafts shared the wide,
swift, and difficult river, but the most important invention
was still to come.

8

Steamboats and Steamboat Towns

The people fasten their eyes upon the coming boat
as upon a wonder they are seeing for the first time.
And the boat is rather a handsome sight, too. She
is long and sharp and trim and pretty; she has two
tall, fancy-topped chimneys. . . . the captain stands
by the big bell.

Mark Twain, *Life on the Mississippi*

Inventors tried many ways to improve river travel. On a
flatboat or keelboat, drifting with the current made the
down-river part of the trip easy, but bringing the boat back
was very hard. As mentioned earlier, flatboats were taken
apart after one trip. Keelboats were rowed or sailed against
the wind. Sometimes, men or horses walked on the shore,
pulling the boats with ropes. The men also sometimes used
long poles to push against the river bottom.

Later, there were paddle wheel boats powered by horses
and oxen. The beasts would walk on a huge wheel that
turned a paddle wheel, pushing the craft up the river. Then,
in the early 1800s, Robert Fulton perfected the steamboat.
The first steamboat reached St. Louis in 1817. It was the

Zebulon M. Pike, named for the soldier and explorer who had died in 1813 in the war against the British. It wasn't long until steamboats were traveling both the Mississippi and Missouri rivers.

Steamboats brought big changes. They connected the frontier more directly with eastern cities. The sound of a steamboat whistle brought townspeople and farmers to the river, eager to see what the boat carried. Steamboats brought fancy cloth that replaced homemade cotton and wool fabric. They brought letters, newspapers, chairs and tables, musical instruments, and new people to town. Show-

Advertisement for the *Zebulon M. Pike.* (State Historical Society of Missouri)

The harvest of Missouri forests was quick and efficient. With
an unlimited supply of trees, the woodsmen didn't see any
reason to replant. When one hill was stripped, they moved
to another. Even without the trees, place names remind us of
the ancient forests. Pineville, Birch Tree, Poplar Bluff, Walnut
Grove, and Maples are a few towns you can visit. Of all trees,
the oak has given its name to the most Missouri places. There
are five sections of Kansas City with the word *oak* in their
names, including Oaks, Oakville, and Oakwood Park. Today's
highway map shows two Oak Groves. One is in Jackson
County and one in Franklin. (State Historical Society of
Missouri)

boats brought actors who put on plays. Steamboats were so
important that the town of Volney, which was twenty miles
from the Missouri River, changed its name to "Fulton" to
honor the steamboat's inventor.

With steamboat travel, more people came to the new
territory seeking wealth and adventure. Tiny river towns
grew up overnight. Portland, in Callaway County, received
its name because it was a natural stopping place on the
Missouri River. Port Perry was the only Mississippi River

port in Perry County. Malta Bend, in Saline County, was named after the steamboat *Malta* ran into a snag and sank there.

Some places on the river were perfect for businesses, and towns grew up around them. Halls Ferry in St. Louis County and Bonnot's Mill in Osage County were each named for a businessman who set up an enterprise by the river.

There are other names from the days of riverboats— the place names used by the captains themselves. In those days, the rivers were wide, shallow, swift running, and swampy. During floods and cave-ins, trees washed down from the banks and stuck in the bottom, becoming a hazard to wooden ships. Naming every bluff, bend, and island helped the captains warn each other about dangers ahead.

Boats also shared the water with giant log rafts. Pine in the forests of the new territory was valuable, and these huge rafts of logs were floated down streams and rivers to market. The lumber men built towns and named them after the trees they cut down and sold: Big Piney, Pineville, and Piney Spring are three. The boatmen and the rafters gave names to all the important places on the rivers and streams. In a few miles of Piney Creek, a rafter would pass a place called McCortney Slide, where a fellow named McCortney had wrecked, then Miller Spring, owned by a farmer named Miller, and Wildcat Shoal, where wildcats had been seen. The rafter had to be careful as he passed Hog Shoal, where the creek was said to "hog" rafts and wreck them, but he could look forward to a long, swift stretch of water known as Sweet Water.

A few miles down the river, he would pass Devil's Elbow, a rocky, swift, and tricky turn in the stream. Today, there is a town at Devil's Elbow known by the same name as the bend in the river.

9

Statehood

The woodland districts are found towards the great
rivers. The interior is composed of vast regions of
naked and sterile plains, stretching to the Shining
Mountains. . . . the country north and south of the
Missouri is necessary each to the other.

—Petition for Missouri statehood
to the U.S. Congress, 1817

Some of Missouri's first settlers came from Kentucky,
Tennessee, Virginia, and the Carolinas. There were so many
settlers from those states that parts of central and northern
Missouri became known as Little Dixie. The settlers brought
familiar names and used them in their new homes. We
have the Missouri towns of Lexington, Richmond, Knox-
ville, Memphis, and Bowling Green. Columbia, Missouri,
was probably named after Columbia, Kentucky, and the
Missouri towns of Paris (pronounced PAIR-iss) and Versailles (pronounced ver-SAYLZ) are named for Kentucky
towns, not the Paris (pronounced par-EE) and Versailles
(pronounced vair-SIGH) in France.

Lincoln County was formed in 1818. It was named by its

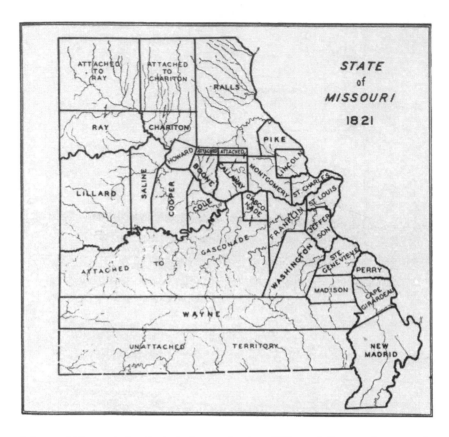

Map of the original state boundaries. When Missouri was admitted to the Union, its counties were divided on the basis of population. (State Historical Society of Missouri)

first citizen, who said, "I was born, sir, in Lincoln County, North Carolina. I lived for many years in Lincoln County, in old Kentucky. I wish to live the remainder of my days and die in Lincoln County, in Missouri."

As the number of people grew, leaders wanted to make the territory into a state. St. Louis had a newspaper published in English and French. The newspaper, the *Missouri*

Gazette, published articles in favor of statehood, exciting much discussion among its readers.

There was a question to answer before statehood could be reached: Would Missouri allow slavery? Half the states at that time allowed slavery and half did not. In 1819, Missouri had about 66,000 residents. Almost 10,000 were African American slaves. Many landowners, who could vote, depended on their slaves for work. Women and slaves could not vote.

Some Missourians wanted to make slavery illegal. Others said the owners had a right to keep their slaves. There was much debate and anger over the issue. The United States government said they would not let a new slave state join the United States, because it would change the balance of slave and free states. Finally there was a solution to the problem. The territory of Maine asked for statehood. Maine did not have slavery. With Maine and Missouri admitted at the same time, there would still be a balance of slave and free states. This solution is known as the Missouri Compromise. In 1821, Missouri became the twenty-fourth state in the Union.

Missouri needed a new state capital. The site at St. Charles was too far from the western border. People wanted a more central location, near the Osage and Missouri rivers, two major transportation waterways.

After government leaders selected the location in central Missouri, they wanted to name the new capital "Missouriopolis." What a mouthful! Finally, the new town became the first in the United States to be named for Thomas Jefferson. "City of Jefferson" is still the official name of Missouri's capital city.

Settlers were attracted to Missouri partly because land

was cheap. One section of Clark County was called "Bit Nation" because land was only twelve and a half cents per acre. Two acres could be bought for two bits, or twenty-five cents.

Missouri had plenty of forests for lumber, game to hunt, cheap land, and mineral resources. With mighty rivers for transportation, the state had all that it needed to grow.

The resources were so rich that some of the pioneer place names seem like advertisements to bring new settlers. Three creeks were named "Beaver Creek" because of the valuable beaver colonies to be found there. Several more creeks were named "Bear Creek," and settlers in Lewis County boasted that they could go out any morning and kill a bear for breakfast.

Hunting for honey could bring good income. The honey bee is not native to North America; it came with the English and spread rapidly with settlement. Beeswax and honey were important to the pioneers and brought income to pioneer families. Some early writers described honey trees where fifty gallons of valuable honey was harvested. At least three Missouri creeks were named "Honey Creek."

In southwest Missouri, the largest pioneer town was Springfield, seat of Greene County. Its name was chosen by voters, who were persuaded by one of the founders. He took each one aside and said, "I was born and raised in a beautiful little town in Massachusetts, and it would please me very much if you would go over and vote to name this town Springfield."

As Missouri's population increased, new trails were developed to take people farther west. Pioneers could begin in St. Louis and travel by steamboat to one of the towns on the Missouri River. There they could find a wagon master. The wagon master would tell the family how to make the

A covered wagon measured four feet by twelve feet. In it, pioneers would carry everything they needed for the trip west and the first months of farming. A pioneer traveling to California was advised to carry two flannel shirts, two wool undershirts, four pairs of wool socks, two pairs of cotton socks, four silk handkerchiefs, two pairs of shoes, two ponchos, one coat, one overcoat, one comb, one brush, two toothbrushes, four pounds of soap, one knife, needles, thread, buttons, pins, a thimble, and some beeswax. The trip took three to six months. (State Historical Society of Missouri)

trip west. They would gather the things they needed, buy a covered wagon, oxen, and horses, and join other families to form a wagon train.

There were three major trails west, each named for the place it went. The Santa Fe Trail, opened in 1822, went to Santa Fe, New Mexico. After 1842, settlers could also choose to travel the Oregon Trail or the California Trail. On the Oregon and California trails, the wagon trains went west through the Rocky Mountains together, then split northwest to Oregon or west to California.

Many Missouri River towns claim to be the first on the

SANTA FE, N. M.

UNITED STATES MAIL.

FROM INDEPENDENCE TO SANTA FE

NEW MEXICO

SEMI-MONTHLY

S ANTA FE Traders, and those desirous
of crossing the Plains to New Mexico,
are informed that the undersigned will
carry the United States Mail, from Independence to Santa Fe, for four years,
commencing on the first day of July, 1857,
in stages drawn by six mules.

The Stages will leave Independence and
Santa Fe on the first and fifteenth of each
month They will be entirely new, and
comfortable for passengers well guarded,
and running through each way, in from
twenty to twenty-five days. Travellers to
and from New Mexico, will doubtless find
this the safest, and most expeditious and
comfortable, as well as the cheapest
mode of crossing the plains.

FARE THROUGH

From November 1st to May 1st.....$150 00
   "   May 1st to November 1st..... 125 00

Provisions, arms and ammunition fur-
nished by the proprietors.

Packages and extra baggage will be
transported when possible to do so, at
the rate of 35 cents per pound in summer,
and 50 cents in winter, but no package
will be charged less than one dollar.

The proprietors will not be responsible
for any package worth more than fifty
dollars, unless contents given and special-
ly contracted for, and all baggage at all
times at the risk of the owner thereof.

In all cases the passage money
must be paid in advance, and passengers
must stipulate to conform to the rules
which may be established by the undersigned, for the government of their line
of stages, and those travelling with them
on the plains.

No passenger allowed more than forty
pounds of baggage in addition to the
necessary bedding.

Mr. Levi Speidleburg, at Santa Fe, and
J & W R. Bernard & Co., at Westport,
Mo., and our conductor and agents are
authorised to engage passengers and re-
ceipt for passage money

HOCKADY & HALL.

July 18, 1857.   n42-tf

Advertisement for stage rides from Independence to Santa Fe in 1857. (from *Kansas City, Missouri: Its History and Its People, 1808–1908*, vol. 1, by Carrie Westlake Whitney [Chicago: S. J. Clarke Publishing Co., 1908])

trail west. Franklin, Arrow Rock, Independence, and Westport all have a right to make the claim. At each, a traveler
would find the tools and goods needed for the trip. By the
1850s U. S. Mail could be sent from Independence to Santa
Fe twice a month.

These towns all illustrate how places get their names.
Franklin, founded in 1816, was named for Benjamin Frank-
lin of Philadelphia, one of the signers of the Declaration of
Independence. Early wagon trains were put together at
Franklin, then crossed the Missouri River on a ferry at
Arrow Rock and went on to Fort Osage and a western trail.
Franklin was flooded in 1827 and rebuilt farther from the
river as New Franklin.

Arrow Rock, founded as a trading post in 1808, was the
site of an old Native American river crossing and meeting
place. According to one story, it was named when a group
of young men competed to win the chief's daughter. In
their contest, they shot arrows into the river to see who

This mural by George Gray, illustrating the Platte Purchase,
was made for the Robidoux Hotel in St. Joseph. (State Historical Society of Missouri)

could shoot the farthest. The winner shot his arrow all the way across the river into a rock on the other side.

The French, hearing this legend, called the place "Pierre à Flèche," which is French for "Arrow Rock." But in 1829, when settlers decided to build a town there, they chose the name "New Philadelphia" in honor of the birthplace of our nation. This name never caught on, and Arrow Rock got its old name back in 1833.

"Independence" is a name that celebrates the high hopes of the early Americans. They saw themselves as building an ideal country, where "life, liberty, and the pursuit of happiness" were everybody's rights.

Ideal names were popular for towns in most of the nineteenth century. There are, for example, Liberty in Clay County, Friendship in Caldwell County, Success in Texas County, and Tranquility in Clark County.

Westport was founded in 1833. By this time, people were moving west in great numbers. Westport was planned by business leaders who thought its nearby river landing would make it the perfect pioneer center. The founders were right. In a five-month period in 1859, 1,970 wagons, 840 horses, 4,000 mules, 15,000 oxen, and 2,300 pioneers left Westport to find new lives.

As the trail towns became successful, developers looked for more river town sites. They wanted more riverfront property, and that meant moving farther northwest along the Missouri River.

Today's Missouri has a shape different from that of the original state because a triangle of land between the Missouri River and the original western boundary has been added in the northwest part of the state. The Platte and Nodaway rivers run through the flat, fertile farmland there.

This was Indian territory, known to Native Americans

The elegant Patee House in St. Joseph was like a modern hotel. It had rooms for 300 guests and banquet rooms for special celebrations. Famous for its luxury and good food, it had many important visitors. (State Historical Society of Missouri)

as "the beginning of the road to paradise." A few Euro-Americans had settled there, however, and it wasn't long before they began asking the state and federal governments to add the land to Missouri.

The federal government bought the property with money and merchandise, promising the Native Americans new hunting lands farther west. In 1836 the last purchases were made, and in 1837 the Platte region was added to Missouri. The new property gave Missouri a longer border along the river and more sites for trading towns.

Trade in Westport and Independence was hurt when a deadly disease came to town in 1849. The cholera epidemic frightened people away. That year was good for a new town in the Platte region. Joseph Robidoux, a fur trader, had founded St. Joseph in 1840. The city is named for his patron saint, and the first streets of the city are named for Robi-

THE PONY EXPRESS
St. JOSEPH, MISSOURI

The Pony Express rider is commemorated by this statue at the Pony Express Museum in St. Joseph. Mail was carried in the pouches that hang from the saddle. (courtesy of Pony Express National Memorial, St. Joseph, Missouri)

doux's children. Thousands of people went west through St. Joseph in 1848 when gold was discovered in California.

For a brief time, St. Joseph was home to the Pony Express, a company started to carry mail to California. Before the Pony Express, a letter sent from St. Louis traveled from one to four months before it arrived in California. The mail went by riverboat to New Orleans, then by ship to Panama. It crossed Panama by railroad, was put on another ship, and sailed to California. If the railroad in Panama was out of order, the mail went all the way around South America.

After the Pony Express was founded in 1860, mail came from St. Louis by steamboat and railroad to St. Joseph, then was carried in mailbags by horseback. Pony Express stations were ten to fifteen miles apart, and riders would gallop from one to the next. At each station, a rider would get a snack of food and a fresh horse; then he would ride to the next stop. Each rider rode one day and night—twenty-four hours—before stopping to rest.

The Pony Express only operated for nineteen months, but its name lives on. Often, you will hear the St. Joseph area referred to as the Pony Express Region.

10

New Settlers from Europe

A small family requires no more than four or five
acres of land to begin with. Half an acre is enough
for garden vegetables . . . after which there are left
three or four acres for corn.
                    —Gottfried Duden, *Report on a Journey to
                    the Western States of North America*

Besides Anglo-American settlers from the East and South,
new groups of European-born immigrants were also moving into Missouri. A few German immigrants came as early
as 1798 to the Cape Girardeau area from North Carolina.
Around 1800 a group of German-speaking pioneers settled
along the Whitewater River in what are now Cape Girardeau and Bollinger counties, where they became known as
the "Whitewater Dutch."

In 1829, a book about Missouri was published in Germany.
It was written by Gottfried Duden, who had lived in Warren
County more than two years. Duden's book described the
beauty of the new land and the need for businessmen and
craftsmen. He reported that farmers had the chance to own
land in Missouri. Thousands of German settlers came, many

of them in organized groups that planned to build German cities.

The Missouri town of Hermann was planned in 1836. Its founders, new immigrants living in Philadelphia, wanted to build a town in the West where Germans could settle and keep their language and traditions. They planned parks, a German school, and churches that would have services in German. The main street, Market Street, was to be ten feet wider than the main street in Philadelphia. They named the new city "Hermann" for a hero who had saved Germany from the Romans almost 2,000 years earlier.

The first settlers found a wilderness on the river. The first winter, they nearly starved, but a few Americans living nearby helped them survive. By 1839, however, they had built ninety houses and laid out the streets according to the plan they had made in Philadelphia. Today, Hermann still has German traditions and a German look.

There are other German towns along the Missouri River. The area is sometimes called the Missouri Rhineland after the beautiful region of Germany along the Rhine River. In Missouri, there is even a town called Rhineland, across the river from Hermann. Rhineland was flooded in 1993, and the people decided to move the town to higher ground.

In 1839, a group of Germans settled in present-day Perry County, south of Ste. Genevieve. They founded seven towns, all named for places in Saxony, Germany: Altenburg, Dresden, Frohna, Johannisberg, Paitzdorf, Seelitz, and Wittenberg.

These settlers started a school, the "Log Cabin College," in Altenburg for both men and women. A coeducational school was a new idea in Missouri at that time. Of the German towns in Perry County, Altenburg remains the largest. By 1980, the official census for Wittenberg was reported as four. The townspeople had to convince census

The town of Dutzow, near Duden's Hill in Warren County, was one of the first German settlements. Dutzow was named by a wealthy landowner after his estate near the Baltic Sea in Germany, and the town's streets were named for German poets. The city became a social center for wealthy immigrants in the early 1830s. (photograph by A. E. Schroeder)

officials that there were, in fact, eight people living in Wittenberg. Johannisberg and Dresden have disappeared, but there is a new Dresden in Pettis County, perhaps named for the Perry County town.

In 1844, another German group settled in Missouri and founded a town. Bethel, in Shelby County, was founded by 500 followers of William Keil, a religious leader who hoped to begin an ideal society. A house was built for each family in the group. Single adults lived in a big house, which also served as a hotel. The settlers shared 3,500 acres of farmland, which the men farmed. Men also worked in the stores, mill, tannery, and tailor's shop, where the men's clothing was made. Women took care of the homes and made the women's clothing.

William Keil led many of the colonists west in 1855, but the Bethel Colony lasted until his death in 1879. When their leader died, the Colony was dissolved and Colony property was divided. Each person received whatever he or she had brought to the group. In addition, each man in Bethel received $7.76 for every year he had spent in the Colony. Each woman received half that amount. Today, over thirty of the Bethel Colony homes and other buildings remain, and the town has many German festivals.

Of all European immigrants, Germans came to Missouri in the largest numbers, but during the nineteenth century, people from many European countries began to settle in the state. There were enough Czechs, Italians, Hungarians, and

During the mid-nineteenth century, German immigrants settled in the old French towns along the Mississippi and founded new towns with German names. (photograph by A. E. Schroeder)

William Keil, founder of Bethel, in Shelby County, called his large brick home "Elim," the name of an oasis where Moses and the Israelites found water on their flight from Egypt. Keil lived outside the village so he could be away from the everyday arguments or "little squabbles" of the community. As a leader, his word was final in all matters. (Jerry Berneche painting)

Polish people for many groups to publish newspapers in their own languages. In Europe, times were hard, and people looked to the new land as a place where their dreams could come true.

Many settlers came from the British Isles. Irish settlers started the towns of Shamrock and St. Patrick. English settlers came to New London, Oxford, and Dover. The Scottish settled in Edinburg, Dundee, Argyle, Caledonia, Glasgow, and many other places. There is even a Scotland County, named by the Scottish surveyor who measured the boundaries.

What about the other Missouri place names that come

from foreign lands? As communications improved, Missourians began to hear about events in far-off places and to name their cities after those places. Some Missourians went to fight in foreign wars and came back to name towns after the places they had seen. Mexico, Vera Cruz, and Buena Vista were all named around the time of the Mexican War. People in the village of Haarville, in Cole County, first named for an early German settler, renamed the town after Taos, New Mexico.

When the California gold rush took many Missourians west in the late 1840s and early 1850s, they returned with new-sounding names, like "California" and "La Plata." At about the same time, the little town of Hog Eye in Vernon County took a western name for itself—"Nevada," pronounced in Missouri "ne-VAY-da." Scholars say that "hog eye" was the name once given to a sunken place in the ground.

Many foreign place names come from countries the settlers admired for their beauty and culture. Italy—the home of Romans—was well known to those who had studied Roman history in school. From Italy came the names of Milan, Venice, and Rome, Missouri. Carthage was named for a North African market center that was important in Roman history. After a special kind of granite was found near Carthage, Missouri, Carthage marble became famous. The capitol building in Jefferson City and the Empire State Building in New York City are both built of Carthage marble.

Some foreign names have caused problems for their towns. During the first and second world wars, Americans tried to get rid of names that sounded like they came from Germany or Japan. The German name of Potsdam in Gasconade County was changed to "Pershing," the name of a World War I general from Missouri, General John J. Pershing. Other towns refused to change their names. Bismarck

The present state capitol, made of steel beams and Carthage
marble, was finished in 1917. When the building was completed under its budget, the governor ordered that the extra
money should be used for art to decorate the building and
grounds. Today, many of Missouri's artistic treasures are
found at the capitol. (State Historical Society of Missouri)

and Kaiser kept their German names, even though some
people wanted to change "Bismarck" to "Loyal" and "Kaiser" to "Success."

Even after the bombing of Pearl Harbor, Japan, Missouri,
kept its name when people learned its story. The town and
its old Catholic church were named for Christians in Japan
who were killed for their faith. The town, and the church,
the "Church of the Holy Martyrs of Japan," kept their
names, but people used to pronounce the name JAY-pan.

11

The Civil War and Change

Oft in dreams I see thee lying
On the battle plain,
Sorely wounded, even dying,
Calling, but in vain.

Weeping sad and lonely,
Hopes and tears are vain.
When this cruel war is over,
Praying that we meet again.

—"When This Cruel War Is Over,"
from H. M. Belden, *Ballads and Songs*

In 1860, Abraham Lincoln was elected President of the United States. Many Southerners feared that Lincoln would take away their right to own slaves. Southern states began to leave, or secede from, the Union. They formed the Confederate States of America. Both the Union and the Confederacy recruited armies. Soon the country was at war.

There is never a good time for a war. Wars destroy homes, schools, roads, and bridges that have taken many years to build. Wars take people away from home. Crops are not

A cannonball from the Civil War is still lodged in a column of the courthouse in Lexington today. In 1861, Lexington was the site of a battle. The town, which had been taken over by Union troops, was surrounded by Confederates. The battle lasted fifty-two hours before the Union soldiers, without food or water, gave up. (photograph by Gerald Massie, State Historical Society of Missouri)

planted, and businesses close their doors. When there is a war, the effects go much further than the number of dead and wounded soldiers. Wars stop progress, and the hardships they cause continue for years. The Civil War came at a very bad time for Missouri and caused bitter divisions in the state.

Missouri's large population of Southerners owned slaves and did not want to lose them. Many of the new European settlers had come to America to find freedom and did not like slavery. Settlers from the northern states were also against slavery. The state was divided by the anger of these two groups.

Some historians wonder if there might have been a way to peacefully solve the problems. There were many issues involved in the Civil War, and people were not willing to try to settle them peacefully.

Missouri's governor, Claiborne Fox Jackson, agreed that people should be able to keep slaves, but he also thought that the Union should stay together. Most Missourians took one side or the other. Many with Southern roots joined the Confederates. Those from the North and a large number of new European immigrants joined the Union. One Little Dixie county withdrew from both the Union and the Confederacy. The story goes that all the young men in the county had left to fight with the South. Then the word came in October 1861 that Union troops were very close. Food and water were important resources, and troops on the march could destroy a family's supplies for the winter.

News passed quickly through the county, and the home guard, made up of boys and old men, joined together to protect their farms. With hunting rifles and logs painted black to look like cast-iron cannons, the group kept the soldiers away. Then the two sides reached an agreement.

The Union commander promised not to bother the county. The home guard promised not to side with the Confederacy. A message was sent to Jefferson City and Washington, D.C., that the county had become a kingdom and would not join either side. Today, we still call Callaway County the Kingdom of Callaway, and the town where peace was made is called Kingdom City.

While there are no towns in Missouri named for Civil War events or people, some place names remind us of those bad years. The area around a little creek south of Springfield was the site of Missouri's bloodiest battle. The creek was named for a nearby landowner, James Wilson, and the battlefield is now a designated historic site named "Wilson's Creek National Battlefield." In 1991, a reenactment of the Battle of Wilson's Creek brought 4,200 reenactors, some from as far away as Canada and France, to commemorate the 130th anniversary of the battle. Over 50,000 people watched the reenactment.

The name of Patty's Cave was well known in Butler County during the Civil War. In Patty's Cave near Cane Creek, Southern sympathizers hid corn, meat, and other provisions from the raiders from the North. The cave was named for John C. Patty, a nearby farmer and blacksmith who had moved from Tennessee to Butler County in the early 1850s.

The Missouri Department of Conservation has named some of its public lands in memory of the Civil War. Bushwhacker Wildlife Area, for example, is near the Kansas border. Outlaws and guerrilla soldiers were known as bushwhackers, or those who shot from the bush. These bands of outlaws raided farms and towns in Kansas and many parts of Missouri.

The word *bushwhacker* could refer to fighters from either

Civil War reenactors. Today, people from all over the world like to dress up as Civil War soldiers and reenact battles. Craftsmen try to make rifles, uniforms, hats, and all the equipment as authentic as possible. (Missouri Division of Tourism photo)

side of the fight, or even to ruffians who cared nothing about either side. These gang members were especially troublesome near the Kansas border. In that area, the bushwhackers were usually Southern sympathizers who raided farms and towns in Kansas and Missouri and then retreated to their homes. Some of them became heroes to other Southerners, who had been attacked by Northern sympathizers, called "Jayhawkers," from Kansas.

As the conflict continued, every family in Missouri was touched by fear or loss. There were more than 1,000 battles in this state. More than 19,000 Missouri men were killed fighting in Missouri and in other places.

Near the end of the war, Missouri was the first state to free its slaves. Soon after, Abraham Lincoln granted freedom to all slaves in the United States.

When peace came, a group of African American soldiers gave their pay to start a college to train teachers for the newly freed black people. Lincoln Institute was founded in 1866. The first classes were held in a leaky log cabin in Jefferson City. Today, Lincoln University welcomes students of all races.

Many freed slaves never left their old homes. Even though they were free, they had no place to go. Others decided to try and make new lives for themselves. Some slave owners gave land so the former slaves would have a place to live. In Ray County, a town named "Fredonia" was planned in 1869 for freed slaves, but it never really developed.

Other African American settlements had more luck. A wooded area called Little Africa in Pike County lasted until the 1930s or 1940s. It had been a hideout for runaway slaves, so it had a history of black settlement. An overgrown cemetery is still on the site.

Another town for freed slaves was Pennytown in Saline County. Pennytown was founded by Joseph Penny, a freed man from Kansas. He came to Missouri to farm and saved enough money to buy eight acres. A blacksmith came to set up shop, and a school and church were built. By 1880, two hundred African American people lived in Pennytown. Like other Missourians, they planted big gardens, kept chickens and hogs, and helped each other with chores like house building, crop harvesting, and quilting. Today the church, now on the National Register of Historic Places, still stands.

This 1910 photograph of Lincoln University shows the early buildings high on a hill. Today, new buildings and parking lots have surrounded these buildings. (Missouri State Archives)

Most African American settlements were in cities. St. Charles had African American sections called Africa Hill, Goose Hill, and Bates Hill. These neighborhoods had many businesses owned by former slaves. There were four African American doctors, three drugstores, three barbers, three restaurants, and three builders who worked in the three communities.

After the Civil War, many schools were built for the African American children. "Lincoln School" was a popular name for these, and Missouri still has at least eighteen Lincoln Schools. In Pike County, there is a park named "Lincoln School Park" on land where there once was a school for black children from Pike County and other nearby counties. When schools were integrated, the building was torn down.

There are eight Missouri schools named "Douglass School" for Frederick Douglass, a slave who became a famous leader, writer, and speaker. Much later came schools named "Carver School" for George Washington Carver, the world-famous scientist who was born a slave. His home was in rural Newton County near the town of Diamond, named because it was near a diamond-shaped grove of trees. Today, the George Washington Carver National Monument in Newton County commemorates Carver's life and work.

12

Towns for Railroads and New Roads

The period immediately following the Civil War was one of wild railroad promotion. Small systems were chartered, promoted, sometimes built, then sold or abandoned. . . . Nevertheless, during this time some of the major rail systems of today got their start.

—Charles van Ravenswaay, *The WPA Guide to 1930s Missouri*

When the Civil War ended, Missouri was able to start to grow again. The first railroad across the state had been completed in 1859, just before the war. It ran between Hannibal on the Mississippi River and St. Joseph on the Missouri.

The Hannibal and St. Joseph Line formed an important link between the eastern United States and the western frontier. The state was ready for more railroads, more people, and more towns when the war was over.

Several Missouri towns and cities were born in the years after the Civil War, and others grew larger. Between 1860 and 1870, the number of people in St. Joseph more than doubled, and the population of St. Louis almost doubled.

Kansas City's population grew to more than seven times what it was in 1860, from 4,418 to 32,260.

Joplin became a boomtown after lead was discovered there in 1870. In three years the town grew to 4,000 people. By 1900, it was a city of 26,000. Joplin was named for the preacher who established the first Methodist church in the area in 1840.

Besides the booming cities, there were a growing number of small towns and new roads. There were little towns named "Stringtown" in twelve places in the state, where a few houses and stores faced the road in a line. Nine towns named "Cross Roads" or "Crossroads" appeared in places where two roads came together. In these country towns, farmers would find places to take care of everyday needs— a general store, a blacksmith, and a mill where corn and wheat could be ground. A church and a school were often built nearby.

In agriculture and commerce, the mule became an important asset. A mule is a cross between a donkey and a horse. Mules are bigger than donkeys, and they can work harder in the heat and need less feed than horses. Missouri farmers bred large work horses to the donkey and produced a big mule, which came to be known as the Missouri mule.

Many towns and counties in Missouri called themselves the Mule Capital of the World. Tarkio, where one breeder lived, was famous for its big round brick barn. Fulton was famous for its Monday mule sales, which brought so much traffic to town that schools were dismissed.

In the late 1800s, post offices were established in many new places. To have a post office, a town had to have a name unlike any other in the state. Cross Roads in Douglas County was first to claim its popular name. Other cross-road towns took other names: South Fork in Howell County,

The Missouri mule became world famous at the Louisiana Exposition in 1904. A cross between a donkey and a horse, the mule combined the best features of both. Mule lovers say that mules are stronger and smarter than horses, but the phrase "stubborn as a mule" wouldn't be said so often if it weren't true. (State Historical Society of Missouri)

Belleview in Iron, Omaha in Putnam, Camburg in Ripley, and Damascus in St. Clair. Some towns named "Crossroads" disappeared. One was actually moved. The houses from Cross Roads in Dade County were moved to Everton when a railroad stop was built there. Because the first "iron horses" needed water and fuel every few miles, new railroad towns were born with every new line.

Railroads were not welcomed by all people in Missouri because they were developed by outsiders. They were supported by tax money but charged high fees to deliver freight. Like the steamboat, however, the railroads were a major improvement in transportation.

At a railroad town, travelers would find all the businesses of a crossroads town, plus some especially for the traveler. There would usually be a restaurant that offered a limited menu each day. Everyone from the train would stop and eat together at meal time. There would be a hotel or two, so both travelers and crew members could spend the night. Later, the dining car and sleeping car made it possible for passengers to spend the whole day on a train.

Early explorers named the waterways, but railroad men named the largest number of Missouri towns. A few are Eldon in Miller County, Monett in Barry County, Slater in Saline County, and Thayer in Oregon County, all named for railroad bosses. Moberly, named for a railroad president, was nicknamed "The Magic City" because it appeared on the prairie almost overnight.

Construction crew for the Missouri, Kansas, and Texas Railroad laying tracks near Rocheport in about 1893. (State Historical Society of Missouri)

The steam engine harnessed the power of boiling water to drive iron wheels on tracks across the prairie, but the first trains needed to stop every five miles to pick up water and fuel. When technology improved, many of the old railroad towns disappeared. (State Historical Society of Missouri)

Helena in Andrew County and Tina (pronounced TY-na) in Carroll County were named after the daughters of railroad men. Marceline in Linn County and Una in Jackson County were named for wives of railroaders.

The town of Mokane in Callaway County has had several name changes. Each tells a little about the town's history. First, as a river town, it was named "Smith's Landing" for a pioneer woman we know only as "Mrs. Smith." After the town was washed away in a flood it was rebuilt and named "St. Aubert." Another flood forced the town to move to high ground, and St. Aubert was reborn as "Mokane" when the Missouri-Kansas-Texas railroad came through.

Another Missouri railroad town is Pacific, in Franklin County, far from the ocean. Pacific was originally named

"Franklin" when it was planned as a stop on the Pacific Railroad, the first railroad west of the Mississippi. Builders planned that the line would go from St. Louis to the West Coast, but in 1853 they ran out of money. At the same time, Franklin leaders learned that there was another Franklin in Missouri. They changed the name of their town to "Pacific." The railroad could then claim that it had reached Pacific—although not the ocean. The line's name was later changed to Missouri Pacific Railroad.

What happens to a railroad town when the railroad no longer needs it? As steam engines became more efficient, many small towns died. Pacific might have died, but it was in a good location for an exit from a highway. St. Louis commuters moved there.

Later Pacific's economy had another boost. Six Flags, a major amusement park, located there, bringing many motels and restaurants. Many little railroad towns are gone, but Pacific is a good-sized community today.

As highway trucks have taken over a large part of transportation, the railroad towns have shrunk or disappeared. Some of the track bed for the Missouri-Kansas-Texas railroad has been made into trails for walking and biking. Little railroad towns on the M-K-T Trail, or Katy Trail, hope to grow again, with businesses that serve hikers and bikers.

13

⟨━━━⟩♦⟨━━━⟩

Resort Towns

How can you enjoy history, mountains, water fun,
big cities and scenery without driving through a
half dozen different states? The answer's easy. . . .
You can find all those things, and a lot more,
by visiting just one state—Missouri.

—Missouri Division of Tourism,
Missouri Travel Guide

Railroads made travel easier. People began to ship farm
products, lumber, and factory-made goods by train. The
railroads brought immigrants to new parts of Missouri and
took rural sons and daughters to cities to seek their for-
tunes. Small train lines linked communities, and people
from one town could work in another.

Railroads also created a new business for the state—
tourism. The tourism business is now one of Missouri's
most important industries. Some railroad lines were built
especially to take city people to resort towns.

Some of the earliest resorts were called "health spas."
Many people visited these spas to drink and bathe in mineral waters and try special diets. Doctors who lived at the

Excelsior Springs gazebo. In early Excelsior Springs, wealthy
tourists drank the mineral waters and relaxed in beautiful
garden settings. (State Historical Society of Missouri)

resorts were constantly developing new ways for guests to
spend money trying to stay young and feel good.

The concern with health was partly a result of the fear of
epidemics. When a contagious sickness was discovered in
a community, people panicked. In fact, between 1895 and
1910, a special town was founded near St. Louis for people
with contagious diseases. The town, with its own post office, was called "Quarantine."

Excelsior Springs was one of the first health spas in

Missouri. It was built in 1880 after some fishermen found water that had an odd taste. They knew the taste came from minerals in the ground. Mineral waters were thought to cure rheumatism, tuberculosis, and other sicknesses. Soon, railroad lines from Kansas City and Chicago came to Excelsior Springs, bringing tourists to the fancy hotels, baths, and swimming pools.

Ponce de Leon, a resort in Stone County, was named in 1882 for the Spanish explorer who spent his life looking for the fountain of youth. *El Dorado* is Spanish for "the golden place," so it would seem that Eldorado in Clark County and El Dorado Springs in Cedar County were named by the Spanish in the 1700s. In truth, Eldorado was founded in 1853, and El Dorado Springs, a resort, was built in 1881. At least fourteen other cities in the United States are named "Eldorado."

Many Ozark towns started as fishing or hunting camps, and people still enjoy them as such. Hollister was carefully planned in 1906 to look like an English village. Visitors coming into town on the train saw a charming hotel across from the station and homes built on the limestone bluffs. Hollister was named for a railroad man who was a friend of the developer.

Many of today's new tourist towns face major roads rather than a railroad station. The automobile has changed the way we travel. Camdenton was built in 1930 after a new road brought tourists to the Lake of the Ozarks. Camdenton was named for Camden County, which was named for an English politician, Earl Camden, who said in 1770 that the colonies should be free from England.

The opportunity to attract tourists sometimes makes people change place names. When it had a chance to be a tourist town, the Johnson County village of Colbern's Spring

Las Vegas? New York? Chicago? No, it's Branson. After country music stars discovered the area, its winding roads and log cabins became big business. (Ozark Marketing Council)

looked for a new name. Electricity was thought to have special healing powers, so Colbern's Spring became Electric Spring.

Another example of name-changing is Lakeview, a town located near two big lakes. It is close to Branson, where many famous singing stars own theaters. The success of Branson, which was named for its first postmaster in 1881, made Lakeview change its name in 1992 to "Branson West."

The study of place names in Missouri shows how important transportation has been to our towns. All but a few towns were born because they were easy to get to. Towns were built at a place to land a canoe, a place to dock a steamboat, a place where two roads crossed, or a place where trains could get service.

Today, every modern highway brings new towns to the land. A few years after they are built, highway exits become crossroad towns with service stations, restaurants, and souvenir stands. Just as rural crossroad towns had necessities for the farmer, highway exits have businesses for the traveler.

Small towns become suburbs when new highways are built to the cities. The farmland between city and town disappears under new housing. Airports near small towns bring hotels, restaurants, and apartment buildings for airline crews and frequent travelers.

Most of today's new cities borrow names from the old. Lake St. Louis was named for the city thirty miles away. Sometimes, however, a subdivision builder will put his own mark on a town by naming streets and buildings after members of his family.

Other times, new names are chosen for sales appeal. Names like "Brook Side," "Country Ridge," or "Lake Sherwood" make a place sound like a peaceful retreat from the busy world.

For the story of a new place name, we can ask the builder. To learn the story of an old place name, we can ask people who have lived in the area for a long time. When we know the name of a place, we learn something about its history.

14

Collecting Names

Belle, Bland, Boss and Doss
Competition, Concord, Leeper and Sleeper
Now ain't it Peculiar
from Aaron to Zwanzig
run the names of Missouri . . .

—James Bogan, "Missouri Litany"

This book mentions only a few of the thousands of place names in Missouri. Other books offer many more names. Like other students of Missouri place names, you might like to start your own collection.

Allen Walker Read, who had studied Iowa names, was the person who got place-name study started in Missouri in 1927, but Missouri's best-known place-name collector was Robert Ramsay, a professor of English at the University of Missouri. His collection includes the work of many of his students.

Another well-known collector, Arthur Paul Moser, was not an academic researcher. In fact, he dropped out of high school in tenth grade, worked all his life, and didn't begin to collect place names until he was retired. At age sixty-seven, he began his research. He spent most of each day at the local library and published booklets of place names on all Missouri counties. His work shows that it's never too late to begin something you want to do.

There are many ways you can classify place names. In this book, names are grouped according to historical eras. Some collectors like to make up their own categories. There are many towns named after people, for example. These can be divided into towns named after politicians, railroaders, early settlers, and so forth.

Another way to classify names is to group them according to words they have in common. There are many names that start with "Saint." Nearly as many start with "Devil." In Boone County, there's Devil's Icebox, the entry to a cave. In Warren County, there is the Devil's Boot Cave. People say that the devil stepped into a hole and left the impression of his boot there. Near Taum Sauk Mountain, there is a narrow passage called Devil's Toll Gate. Our rivers have dangerous spots called Devil's Elbow and Devil's Race Ground. Missouri's devil also has plenty of places to clean up—Devil's Washpan, Devil's Washboard, and Devil's Wash Basin.

Another classification system is alphabetical. We could look for all the names that start with a certain letter—"X," for example. There are only two we have found in Missouri history, both "Xenia." They may have been named after the town Xenia, Ohio. Xenia was one of the first towns in Nodaway County, but it has disappeared, while the new Xenia, in Putnam County, remained. The original Greek meaning of the word *xenia* is "friendly hospitality."

While "X" was never a popular letter, "Z" has been a winner. Zwanzig, which is German for "twenty," was named for a local man in Morgan County. It had a post office from 1895 to 1901. The settlement of Zell is named after a German town, but no one knows which one. The place name "Zell" can be found in many parts of Germany.

There was a town called Zebra in Camden County. Some say it was named for striped rocks on the bluffs, but it was probably named after a person named Ziebar. Now Zebra lies under the Lake of the Ozarks. There was a Zeta in Stoddard County, named for a letter of the Greek alphabet. Two towns with short names, Zif and Zig, in Stoddard and Adair counties, were named for popular citizens.

Many places are named for the men who built our country. The counties of Washington, Monroe, Jefferson, Polk, and Buchanan are named after U.S. presidents. One president, Andrew Jackson, has two counties named for him, Jackson and Hickory. Jackson's nickname was "Old Hickory."

On the day Daniel Boone died in 1820, a county was being formed in central Missouri. It was named Boone County. Thomas Hart Benton, one of our first U.S. senators, was honored with many place names—Benton County, Benton City, and Benton, the county seat of Scott County. Ramsay found thirty-seven places in Missouri with "Benton" in the name—creeks, parks, schools, and townships.

Some names, like "Springfield," "Paradise," and "Columbia," are found all over the United States. Others are found only in Missouri. "Hocomo" is a name created from the first two letters of each word in "Howell County, MO." "Taneycomo" is from "Taney County, MO."

The study of Missouri place names will never be finished because the population is always shifting. Old towns disappear and new ones are founded. The Ramsay collection, which is housed at the Western Historical Manuscript Collection at Ellis Library, University of Missouri–Columbia,

Sponsors of the M-K-T dream of a trail across the nation, with restaurants and hotels in some of the towns along the way. Most of the trail in Missouri is completed. (Katy Trail Promotions)

has more than 30,000 names. A 1991 study has found over
25,000 other names. This collection is now on computer at
the Department of Geography at the University of Missouri–
Columbia and at the U.S. Geological Survey office in Res-
ton, Virginia.

At the end of this book is a list of books about Missouri
names. There is also an index of all the names in this book
and the pages on which they appear. In the index, we have
included our modern county names after the town. For
example, "Tarkio (Atchison)" means the name of the town
is "Tarkio," and it is located in what is today called Atchison County. "Tarkio," by the way, is a mystery name.
Local people say it may be an American Indian name for
"walnut," but language experts say it is not. "Tarkio" may
be the name of a person or a version of another word or
name. We may never know.

There is plenty to learn about Missouri place names.
Maybe you'll be the next person to discover the history of a
Missouri place name. If you do, please write the Western
Historical Manuscript Collection, 23 Ellis Library, Columbia, MO 65201. Tell us the name and how you learned
about it. Maybe we'll put your story in our next place-
name book.

For More Reading

The Journals of Lewis and Clark, by Meriwether Lewis and William Clark, have been edited into modern language by John Bakeless (New York: Penguin Books, 1964), making it fun and easy to read about the journey in the explorers' own words.

Indians and Archaeology of Missouri, by Carl and Eleanor Chapman (Columbia: University of Missouri Press, 1983), is a classic book about the area's first inhabitants.

"Interesting Missouri Place Names, I and II," edited by Gerald Cohen (Rolla, Missouri: Published by the Editor, 1982 and 1987), is available at most libraries. Cohen includes letters from friends and fellow collectors in his books, so they read like a warm conversation between friends.

The Heritage of Missouri, by Duane Meyer (St. Louis: River City Publishers, 1982), gives a complete, illustrated history of the state and includes a nice chronology, or list of important events and their dates.

Our Storehouse of Missouri Place Names, by Robert L. Ramsay (Columbia: University of Missouri, 1952; reprinted by the University of Missouri Press 1973, 1985, 1988, 1991), gives the most complete list of Missouri place names and includes chapters on Missouri poetry featuring names and name trivia.

The WPA Guide to 1930s Missouri, by Charles van Ravenswaay (Lawrence: University Press of Kansas, 1986), is a reprint of *Missouri, A Guide to the "Show-Me" State* (New York: Duell, Sloan and Pearce, 1941). It gives details of the writer's trips across Missouri in the 1930s. This book is a treasure for Missouri place-name studies, history, and sight-seeing.

Arthur Paul Moser wrote so many booklets about Missouri place names that it is impossible to list them all. Readers will probably want to begin with the booklets about the counties nearby, but might want to read them all someday. Your public library can obtain information about the booklets from the Missouri State Library in Jefferson City or the State Historical Society of Missouri in Columbia.

Index

About the Author

Margot Ford McMillen is a native of Chicago. She moved to Callaway County in 1972. She teaches at Westminster College, where she is faculty advisor for the literary magazine. She also publishes an educational magazine called *Our Missouri* and writes articles for other magazines. For many years, her special interests have been Missouri folklife, place names, oral history, conservation, and education.

McMillen lives on a farm in Callaway County with her husband, Howard Marshall, and two dogs named Minnie and Jennings. She has two daughters, Holly and Heather Roberson, and two stepsons, Sandy and John Marshall. Her hobbies are horseback riding and reading. She has a horse named Ben.

Margot Ford McMillen. (photograph by Philip D. Sachs)